Math Counts

Capacity

Introduction

In keeping with the major goals of the National Council of Teachers of Mathematics Curriculum and Evaluation Standards, children will become mathematical problem solvers, learn to communicate mathematically, and learn to reason mathematically by using the series Math Counts.

Pattern, Shape, and *Size* may be investigated first—in any sequence.

Sorting, Counting, and *Numbers* may be used next, followed by *Time, Length, Weight,* and *Capacity.*

Ramona G. Choos, Professor of Mathematics, Senior Adviser to the Dean of Continuing Education, Chicago State University; Sponsor for Chicago Elementary Teachers' Mathematics Club

About this Book

Mathematics is a part of a child's world. It is not only interpreting numbers or mastering tricks of addition or multiplication. Mathematics is about *ideas.* These ideas have been developed to explain particular qualities such as size, weight, and height, as well as relationships and comparisons. Yet all too often the important part that an understanding of mathematics will play in a child's development is forgotten or ignored.

Most adults can solve simple mathematical tasks without the need for counters, beads, or fingers. Young children find such abstractions almost impossible to master. They need to see, talk, touch, and experiment.

The photographs and text in these books have been chosen to encourage talk about topics that are essentially mathematical. By talking, the young reader can explore some of the central concepts that support mathematics. It is on an understanding of these concepts that a child's future mastery of mathematics will be built.

Henry Pluckrose

1995 Childrens Press® Edition
© 1994 Watts Books, London, New York, Sydney
All rights reserved.
Printed in the United States of America.
Published simultaneously in Canada.
1 2 3 4 5 6 7 8 9 0 R 04 03 02 01 00 99 98 97 96 95

Math Counts

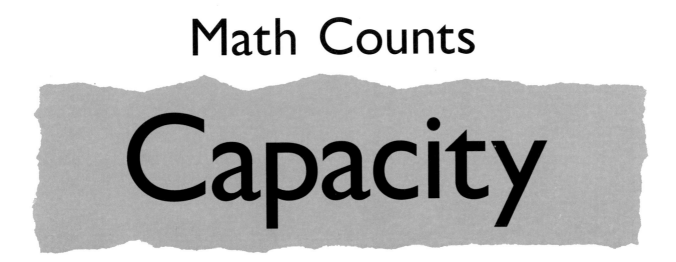

Capacity

By Henry Pluckrose

Mathematics Consultant: Ramona G. Choos,
Professor of Mathematics

 CHILDRENS PRESS®
CHICAGO

Have you ever played with damp sand,
packed it into a pail

and made a sand castle?
Why does the sand
take the shape of the pail?

A pail, a thimble, an egg cup,
a jar, and a box are containers.
Containers hold things.
Inside a container there is a space.

6

The space inside a container can hold solids, liquids, or just air.

Here are some containers.
If you filled each of them
with water,

can you guess which would hold the most
and which would hold the least?

It is sometimes easy to guess which container will hold the most water when they are different sizes.

It's much more difficult to guess
when the containers look almost the same.

Guessing can be difficult.
Which of these two containers
holds the most?
We must measure to find out.

Pour water from the jug
into the dish.
What does this tell you?

Now collect some empty containers.
How can you tell
which one will hold the most water
and which one will hold the least?

We do not have to use water.
We could use sand or marbles instead.
The sand fills all the space in the jar.
Do the marbles fill all the space?

Often we need to measure exactly.
We may use the liter as a standard measure
for liquids.
Or we may use pints, quarts, and gallons.
Many drinks are sold both ways

and so are many other things.

17

A liter is quite a large measure. Smaller quantities are measured in deciliters or milliliters.

A quart is quite a large measure, also. Smaller quantities are measured in pints, cups, or ounces.

18

Ten deciliters make a liter.
A thousand milliliters make a liter.
Two cups make a pint.
Two pints make a quart.

Standard measures are important.
The ingredients for a cake
have to be mixed in the right quantities.

Garden fertilizers have to be carefully measured.

Medicines must be measured carefully when they are made

and when we take them.

23

Standard measures help us to measure exactly. When a driver buys a liter, or a gallon, of gasoline, she knows exactly how much she will get wherever she buys it.

The gasoline runs from the pump
into the car's gas tank.
When the tank is full, it will hold no more gas.
Capacity is the word used to describe
the most that a container can hold.

Some containers are very large.
This tanker holds many liters, or gallons.

These drums hold chemicals.
Which container has the greater capacity,
a tanker or a drum?

Being able to measure capacity
is important.
What might happen to this ship
if too much coal was loaded into it?

What might happen to this reservoir if too much water went into it?

Capacity is not the same as weight.
The stones fill the jar and so does the water.
Which do you think is heavier?

Capacity is a word we use to describe space,
even when the space is empty.

31

Library of Congress Cataloging-in-Publication Data

Pluckrose, Henry Arthur.
    capacity / Henry Pluckrose.
       p.   cm.
    Originally published: London; New York: F. Watts, 1988.
    (Math counts)
    Includes index.
    ISBN 0-516-05451-1
       1. Volume (Cubic content) — Juvenile literature. [1. Volume (Cubic content) 2. Weights and
    measures.] I. Title.
    QC104.P58   1995
    530.8 — dc20   94-38005
                                                                              CIP
                                                                              AC

Photographic credits: Chris Fairclough, 4, 5, 6, 7, 8, 9, 10, 11, 12, 13, 14, 15, 16, 17, 19, 20,
21, 23, 24, 25, 27, 28, 30, 31; Unicorn Stock Photos: © Betts Anderson, 18, © Tommy Dodson,
22; ZEFA, 26; Viewfinder, 29
Editor: Ruth Thomson
Assistant Editor: Annabel Martin
Design: Chloë Cheesman

INDEX

air, 7
capacity
    defining, 25, 31
    importance of measuring, 28, 29
containers, 8
    capacity of, 25, 27
    defining, 6
    filling, 4-5
    shape of, 12, 13
    size of, 8, 9, 10, 11, 26
    space inside, 7
cooking, standard measures in, 20
cups, 18, 19
deciliters, 18, 19
drums, 27
gallons, 16, 24
gardening, standard measures in, 21
gasoline, measuring, 24-25

heavy, 30
large, 26
less, 14, 15
light, 30
liquids, 7
liters, 16, 18, 19, 24
medicines, measuring, 22-23
milliliters, 18, 19
more, 14, 15
ounces, 18
pints, 16, 18, 19
quarts, 16, 18, 19
reservoir, 29
small, 26
solids, 7
space, 31
standard measures, importance of, 20, 21, 22, 23, 24
tankers, 27
weight, 30